Cities through Time

Daily Life in Ancient and Modern

ATHENS

by Dawn Kotapish

illustrations by Bob Moulder

RP

Runestone Press/Minneapolis
An imprint of Lerner Publishing Group

The *Cities through Time* series is produced by Runestone Press, an imprint of Lerner Publishing Group, in cooperation with Greenleaf Publishing, Inc., Geneva, Illinois.

Text design by Melanie Lawson and Jean DeVaty
Cover design by Michael Tacheny

Runestone Press
An imprint of Lerner Publishing Group
241 First Avenue North
Minneapolis, Minnesota 55401 U.S.A.

Website address: www.lernerbooks.com

Library of Congress Cataloging-in-Publication Data

Kotapish, Dawn.
    Daily life in ancient and modern Athens / Dawn Kotapish;
illustrated by Bob Moulder.
        p. cm. — (Cities through time)
    Includes index.
    Summary: A historical exploration of events and daily life in
Athens in both ancient and modern times.
    ISBN 0–8225–3216–6 (lib. bdg. : alk. paper)
    1. Athens (Greece)—Social life and customs—Juvenile literature.
[1. Athens (Greece)] I. Moulder, Bob. ill. II. Title. III. Series.
DF275.K66 2001
949.5'12—DC21   99–10711

Manufactured in the United States of America
2 3 4 5 6 7 – JR – 07 06 05 04 03 02

0432

Contents

Introduction 5

THE RISE OF ATHENS
Early Athens...6
Athens's Agora 8
A Growing City 10
Athenians and Religion..................................12
Stitchers of Songs...14
The Olympic Games......................................16
Solon's Laws...18

CLASSICAL TIMES
Democracy Begins 21
What Athenians Wore 22
Athenians at Home 24
Slaves and Children..26
War and Feasts 28
The Hoplite Soldiers 30
Masters of the Sea..33

THE GOLDEN AGE OF ATHENS
Athens at its Height 34
An Artisan's Life 36
School Days 38
Athens's Great Minds 40

HELLENISM CONQUERS THE WORLD
Athens Falls to the Macedonians 43
Athens under Roman Rule 44
A Day at the Theater 46
Athens Becomes Christian.............................49
Village Life 51

THE LATER YEARS
Turkish Occupation 52
Fight for Freedom 54
After Independence 56
Modern Athens 58

Athens Timeline 60
Books about Greece and Athens 62
Index 63
About the Author and Illustrator 64

Introduction

Athens is the capital of Greece, a southeastern European nation on the Mediterranean Sea. A beautiful, mountainous country, Greece boasts hundreds of islands and 9,000 miles of shoreline. The Aegean Sea, part of the Mediterranean, separates Greece from Asia. Athens sits near the Aegean coast on Attica, a peninsula about 40 miles wide and 50 miles long. Mountains ring the city, where sleek high-rises share the skyline with crumbling ancient structures.

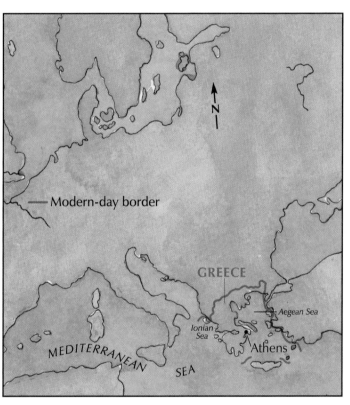

— Modern-day border

GREECE

Ionian Sea

Aegean Sea

MEDITERRANEAN SEA

Athens

Athens began as a small village, but by the fifth century B.C., Athens was a Mediterranean power. The Athenian navy ruled the sea, and Athens was a major trade center. Democracy—the system of government in which citizens vote to make political decisions—flowered in Athens. But Athens was destined to become a conqueror's prize. In the fourth century B.C., King Philip II, father of Alexander the Great, led the Macedonians (Greek-speaking people from north of Athens) to overtake the city. Alexander the Great spread Athenian culture across parts of Europe, North Africa, and Asia. Roman rule followed in 148 B.C., and Athens continued to be a cultural and intellectual center. Athens was swept into the Ottoman Empire from the fifteenth century until 1832, when the city was named capital of a new nation—Greece.

Over the centuries, Athens's art, architecture, philosophy, literature, and politics have deeply influenced the Western world—and continue to do so.

Modern Athens (*opposite*) spills out over the rocky landscape below the Acropolis.

Early Athens

About 5000 B.C., Stone Age herders built simple huts at the top of the Acropolis, a massive limestone hill that stands in the center of modern Athens. They may have originated the name "Athens," a word not of Greek origin. The first Greek-speaking people, the Mycenaeans, emigrated to the area that would become Greece. Soon the Mycenaeans occupied the entire region as well as the Mediterranean island of Crete. Around 1250 B.C., the Mycenaeans arrived in Athens, about 100 miles from their capital of Mycenae.

Early Athenians may have worshiped nature in caves in the cliff. In a cleft at the Acropolis's center, they dug a deep, stair-lined well for water. Steep walls protected

The Acropolis, which means "highest city"

the settlement, which was ruled by a king. The Dorians, a fierce people from northern Greece, overran the region in 1100 B.C. but spared the well-defended city of Athens. In 1200 B.C., Mycenaean culture collapsed and the Greek Dark Ages began. Mycenaean writing was forgotten, and some cities were abandoned. But by 800 B.C., Athens rebounded as a powerful polis, or city-state, with a sizable population.

A Royal Sacrifice

Legend says that the Dorians tried to take Athens, but a prophecy foretold that the Dorians would lose if they killed Athens's king. So the king of Athens disguised himself as a peasant, went to the Dorian camp, and provoked some soldiers into killing him. When the Dorians learned they had killed the Athenian king, they lost heart and gave up trying to conquer Athens.

Athens's Agora

As Athens grew, the Acropolis became overcrowded. People moved to the land surrounding the hill, which remained the site of religious temples. The Agora—a wide-open space in the middle of town—was the heart of the city.

The government forbade people to build permanent houses or shops in the Agora, but merchants and artisans set up temporary stalls where they sold their produce and crafts. Farmers from the countryside sold olives and other farm produce in one section of the Agora. Herders sold donkeys, oxen, pigs, and sheep in another area. Shoppers could buy everything from wine and weapons to slaves in the marketplace.

The Agora was ringed by narrow streets lined with shops, government offices, temples, and public buildings, such as sports centers and stadiums. Nearby, small homes were built around courtyards. At one end of the Agora, a long building with a roof held up by pillars housed more merchants' stalls. The center of the crowded, noisy Agora was a gathering place for the men of Athens, who usually shopped for their households.

The countryside beyond the congested city was also part of Athens. Quiet farms covered the hillsides. Tiny villages of crude stone homes were strung along dirt roads. Eventually Athens extended over the entire Attica peninsula.

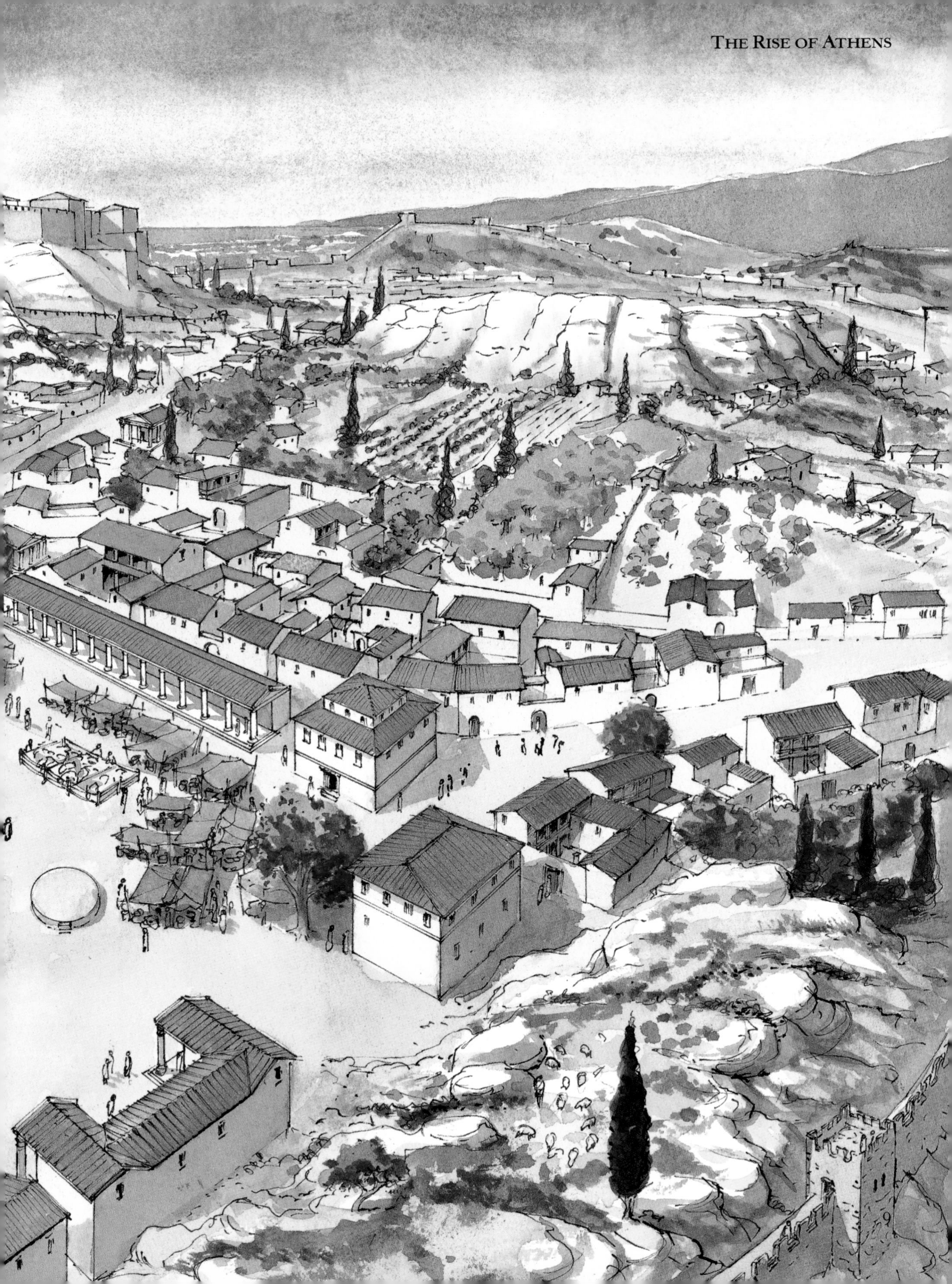

A Growing City

By the late seventh century B.C., the city's population soared. So did the importance of farming and intercity trade.

The Greeks considered farming a noble pursuit. The great Athenian scholar Aristotle once wrote that agriculture "should be ranked first [among professions] because it is just." Most farmers, however, lived less than noble existences. They rented their land from wealthy Athenian landlords and often could keep little of what they produced. Some farmers who couldn't pay off their debts were sold into slavery.

Yet Athenian farmers loved and respected their land. They worked long days and lived simply. Most raised the grapes and olives that thrived in Greece's sandy soil and mild climate. Athenians loved grapes, which they ate fresh and also used to make wine. They crushed the grapes by foot and stored the juice until it fermented into wine. People ate olives or made them into olive oil, which Athenians used for cooking, beauty products, and lamp fuel.

Athens's mountainous terrain was

unsuitable for growing enough grain to make bread for everyone. So Athenian merchants began to trade wine, olive oil, painted pottery, and silver for wheat and barley from Egypt and Russia. They also imported spices, hides, timber, copper, iron, and slaves.

With trade booming out of the nearby port of Piraeus, which was connected to Athens by road, Athenians became master sailors. Merchant ships were about 100 feet long and could be navigated with sails or oars. A typical ship could travel 50 to 60 miles a day. Many men became sailors. But in those days—long before the invention of the compass—sailing across the broad Mediterranean Sea could be dangerous. The Greeks usually tried to hug the coast, keeping land in sight. Even so, many merchant ships were lost to the bottom of the sea.

Walled roadway connecting to Athens

Athenians and Religion

Athenians believed in many gods and goddesses to whom they appealed for advice and for protection from war, disease, and human hardship. Athenians prayed before meals, court proceedings, and government sessions. Athenian children first learned about religion through Greek myths told by storytellers and family members. Chronicles of life on Mount Olympus (a real mountain that was the gods' legendary home) produced colorful, entertaining tales. The Athenians saw their gods as beings who differed little from humans. Gods exhibited the full range of human behaviors, including rage, jealousy, revenge, and selfishness—but the gods were immortal.

Children participated in family religious rituals at an altar in their homes' courtyards. The head of the household (the oldest living male) led the family's religious observances. Sometimes he poured a libation (an offering of food and wine) upon the altar in order to please a deity and to encourage him or her to answer the family's prayer.

Athenians built many temples to honor their gods and goddesses. The Parthenon, a temple built in the fifth century on top of the Acropolis, housed a colossal statue of the city's patron goddess, Athena. The ivory-covered wooden statue was 39 feet tall, with glittering gemstones for eyes. The statue wore a golden robe that weighed 2,500 pounds. The Athenians believed that Athena provided their city with special protection. To ensure that her protection continued, the Athenians made sacrifices of goats, sheep, or birds. During these rituals, Athenians burned part of the animal on the altar to

An ancient statue of Zeus *(right),* king of the gods, as he prepares to launch a thunderbolt. Ancient pottery art *(above right)* shows a family observing religious rituals at home.

please the god or goddess, then ate the rest of the meat. Priests and priestesses, appointed by election or birth, served in the temples. At times, young boys and girls were selected to help the clergy by serving as acolytes, or assistants. The position honored a child's family.

Gods and Goddesses

The Greeks worshiped many gods and goddesses. There were twelve primary deities believed to live on Mount Olympus, Greece's highest mountain. They were:

Zeus, king of the gods
Hera, wife of Zeus and goddess of marriage
Aphrodite, goddess of love and beauty
Apollo, god of light, truth, and music
Ares, god of war
Artemis, goddess of the hunt and youth
Athena, goddess of wisdom, justice, and warfare
Demeter, goddess of grains and fruit
Dionysus, god of wine and fertility
Hephaestus, the gods' blacksmith
Hermes, the divine messenger
Poseidon, god of the sea

Stitchers of Songs

Storytelling answered Athenians' need for entertainment and preserved the stories of their history. Early Athenians listened to the stories of the bards (storytellers), known in Greek as the "stitchers of songs."

Crowds gathered in the Agora and at parties to hear bards recite long, detailed stories and poems from memory. Some bards could recite for hours at a time. Bards accompanied their words by strumming on a lyre or a lute, two popular string instruments. Dressed in flowing robes and sporting beards, the bards

A bard plays a lyre while telling his tale.

spoke carefully to demonstrate respect for the stories.

The greatest Greek bard was a poet named Homer, who is believed to have been blind. Homer may have been born in Athens, although six other cities also claim him as their own. Scholars believe that Homer lived at the end of the Greek Dark Ages in the eighth century B.C.

Homer created two great literary works, the *Iliad* and the *Odyssey*. Gods and monsters play big parts in these heroic tales, parts of which may be based on historical fact. But although Homer is credited as their author, he probably did not invent these stories himself. They most likely have roots in the myths and legends of the Mycenaean age.

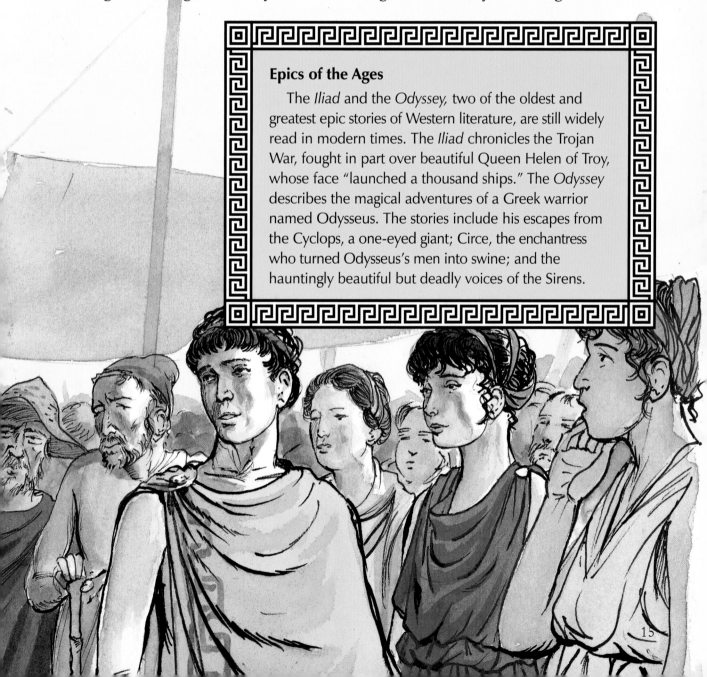

Epics of the Ages

The *Iliad* and the *Odyssey,* two of the oldest and greatest epic stories of Western literature, are still widely read in modern times. The *Iliad* chronicles the Trojan War, fought in part over beautiful Queen Helen of Troy, whose face "launched a thousand ships." The *Odyssey* describes the magical adventures of a Greek warrior named Odysseus. The stories include his escapes from the Cyclops, a one-eyed giant; Circe, the enchantress who turned Odysseus's men into swine; and the hauntingly beautiful but deadly voices of the Sirens.

The Olympic Games

Athenians loved sports and athletic competition. The process of developing both a sound mind and a sound body was a central element of Athenian culture. The Greek motto that a socially undeveloped person "could neither swim nor spell" shows that people were judged by both their mental and physical abilities.

The men of Athens attended a gymnasium every day. Here they participated in physical exercises and sports, including running, boxing, wrestling, calisthenics, chariot racing, and throwing the discus and spear. With the exception of chariot racers, all players were nude. Athens's finest athletes trained hard for the Olympic Games. Held every four years, the games were so important that warring city-states called a truce when it was time for the Games. Spectators of the Olympic Games may have numbered as many as twenty thousand men and boys at a time.

Young boys competed in footraces, wrestling matches, and the long jump after the main events of the Olympic Games. Women and girls were forbidden to watch or to take part in the Olympic Games. But every four years, a competition called the Heraia (named for the goddess Hera) was held for female athletes.

At other times, Athenian women enjoyed the game of knucklebone, which was played with the anklebones of cows or goats. The participants tossed the little bones into the air one at a time and tried to catch them on the back of their hands.

Chariot races *(below)* were popular in early Olympic Games. Knucklebone *(right)* was one of the everyday games played in the street or courtyard.

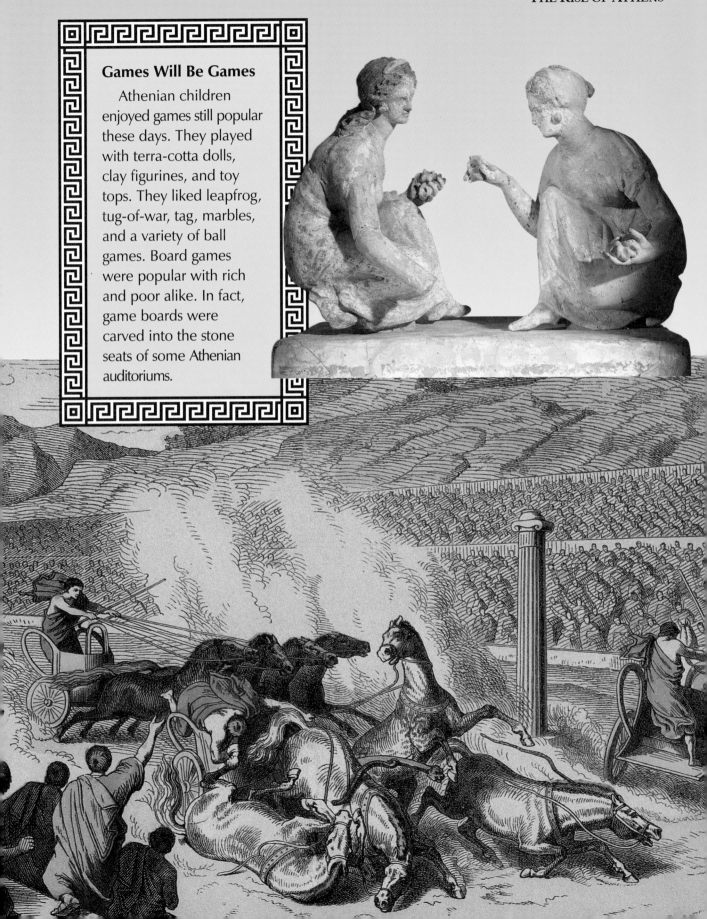

Games Will Be Games

Athenian children enjoyed games still popular these days. They played with terra-cotta dolls, clay figurines, and toy tops. They liked leapfrog, tug-of-war, tag, marbles, and a variety of ball games. Board games were popular with rich and poor alike. In fact, game boards were carved into the stone seats of some Athenian auditoriums.

Solon's Laws

Most Athenian men were farmers, merchants, or skilled workers. Women managed the homes and raised children. The aristocracy ruled early Athens. But by the seventh century B.C., kings had been replaced by a board of nine officers, called archons. Noblemen appointed the archons. After their time of rule was up, archons became life members of the Areopagus, a council that met on the Hill of Ares in Athens.

Some archons were severe. Draco, who ruled in 621 B.C., established harsh penalties for law-breaking. He was the first to write down the laws of Athens.

A reform-minded leader, Solon, was appointed as archon in 594 B.C. Solon was a just and distinguished scholar and poet. He abolished many of the Draconian laws, canceled agricultural debts and mortgages, and freed some farmers who had been enslaved for not paying their debts. He encouraged Athenians who had fled the city to return home again. By showing people that it was possible for political changes to make life better, Solon helped to lay the ground for a new political system, which would be called democracy.

Council members of the Areopagus debated Athenian issues, as seen in this nineteenth-century illustration *(above)*. Solon *(left)*, one of Athens's great archons, relaxed many laws and encouraged political participation.

To the people I have given such privilege as is enough, Neither taking away nor adding to their honor; While those who had power and were famed for their wealth, For them I took care they should suffer no injury. I stood, holding out my strong shield over both, And I did not allow either to triumph unjustly.

—Solon

The boule

We alone regard a man who takes
no interest in public affairs not as a
harmless, but as a useless, character.
—Pericles, Athenian statesman

Democracy Begins

The Areopagus remained for many years, but by the fifth century B.C., it was stripped of its political power. A leader named Cleisthenes helped create a new system, democracy (which means "rule of the people"). It was based on the direct participation of citizens.

But citizenship was open only to adult males with Athenian parents. In the mid-fifth century B.C., voting citizens totaled only about one-sixth of the adult population of Athens. Women, slaves, and the city's resident foreigners could not participate. But democracy still gave rights to more people than had the monarchies or tyrannies of Athens's earliest years.

Athens had two main governing bodies—the boule and the Assembly. The boule had about five hundred members, chosen by lot. The members drafted laws that were later voted on by the Assembly, and they met in the Bouleuterion, a building on the edge of the Agora. All Athenian citizens could participate in the Assembly, which met to decide on laws and issues of city life and foreign policy.

In order for the Assembly to make certain decisions, six thousand citizens had to be present. If that number didn't show up, police retrieved missing citizens from the nearby Agora and swatted them with ropes dipped in red paint to brand them for shirking their civic duty. Assembly participation was considered a privilege and a duty. Because of its large size, the Assembly met outside the city on a hill called the Pnyx. The Assembly met about forty times a year. Each member was allowed one vote and the freedom to speak his mind.

21

What Athenians Wore

Rich or poor, all women spun and wove, a complicated and lengthy process that was responsible for clothing nearly every Athenian. Women first washed wool or flax, combed the fibers, and dyed them with pigments made from earth and plants. Next they spun the wool or flax into thread using a spindle, a shaft of wood with a metal spike on one end and a handle on the other, and a distaff (onto which the thread was wrapped).

Using the thread, women wove cloth on large vertical wooden looms. With the cloth, women produced clothes for every family member, as well as other fabric items for the home, such as cushions, curtains, and wall hangings.

Fortunately for the weavers, people wore simple clothes in Athens's warm climate. From a rectangular length of woven cloth, a woman made a loose tunic called a chiton, a tube of wool or linen cloth held at the waist with a cord. Men and boys wore bleached white or undyed chitons cut above the knee. Women and girls wore ankle- or floor-length chitons bleached white or dyed in various colors. A himation—a long swath of woolen cloth—was worn draped over the chiton. A well-draped himation was a sign of stylishness.

Most Athenians went barefoot, although some wealthier people wore leather sandals outdoors. Men typically sported beards and short hair. Women tied scarves, ribbons, or nets in their hair and wore jewelry. Women also softened their skin with olive oil, reddened their cheeks with rouge, and used a metallic stain imported from Egypt to darken their eyebrows.

In their gracefully draped clothing, Greek women looked elegant while drawing water at the local well.

ΝΗΙΔΕΣΙ ΚΡΗΝΗ Η

Fashion Statements

Because they were handmade from handwoven wool, the chiton and the himation were very valuable. When an Athenian exercised or bathed, he or she had to keep a close eye on these articles of clothing, which were hot items among thieves. In fact, some thieves actually stole himations off people's backs as they walked down the street.

> *Your business will be to stay indoors and help dispatch the servants…when wool is delivered to you, you will see that garments are made for those that need them, and take care that the dried grain is kept ready for eating. And there is another of your duties which I'm afraid may seem to you rather thankless— you will have to see that any of the servants who is ill gets proper treatment.*
> — An Athenian woman's role as described by Xenophon

Athenians at Home

The home was the most important unit of Athenian society and was run like a miniature polis. Husbands and wives made many decisions together, but the man was the head of the family. He oversaw finances and the education of the boys. Mothers taught girls how to run the household. The average Athenian woman was married to a man of her father's choice when she was a teenager. The groom was usually in his late twenties.

Weddings began with prayers and a feast at the bride's parents' house. Later, a horse-drawn wagon took the bride and groom to the groom's house amidst a cheerful procession of family, friends, musicians, and dancers. A torch lit at the woman's childhood home was carried to

her husband's house. A woman couldn't have access to much money, own property, or go to the marketplace or theater alone. But women had many responsibilities in the home, including managing household slaves.

Typical Athenian houses were simply built and simply furnished. They included separate quarters for men and women, usually on separate floors. Men lounged in the andron, the most decorative room in the house. Instead of the wooden or dirt floors of the other rooms, the andron might have a fancy tile floor. Women stayed in the gynaeceum, weaving cloth or socializing. Furniture was limited to benches and low couches, where people ate and sat during the day and slept at night.

Most Athenian homes lacked running water or plumbing. Women or slaves retrieved water from an outside well. A simple pot in the bathroom served as the toilet, which had to be emptied by hand.

Slaves and Children

In 430 B.C., slaves made up about one-third of the city's entire population of 115,000 people. A wealthy family might have had twenty slaves working in their household. Even most poor families owned at least one slave. Slaves performed most household duties and chores involved in manufacturing and commerce. Household slaves did most chores around a house. Female slaves and poorer women fetched water from the household well or the nearest public fountain, where women chatted and shared news. Female slaves or poorer women also did the family's cooking, using terra-cotta pots set over a charcoal fire or portable clay ovens.

Slaves were sold in the Agora. Most slaves were non-Greeks who had been kidnapped by pirates, had been taken as prisoners of war, or had slave parents. Some were Athenian orphans.

On the whole, slaves received just treatment. If slaves were mistreated by their master, they could take refuge at the temple of Theseus or at a religious altar in the city. The owner would be required to sell the slave to someone else. Many slaves developed close ties with their masters and were considered family members. Some received small wages or their freedom. Former slaves couldn't

A Fateful Choice

Children were expensive to raise, and few Athenian parents could support a family of more than one or two kids. A newborn's father decided whether the infant should be allowed to live. The choice was based on the baby's health and the family's economic situation. Most Athenian fathers welcomed their newborns with joy, but some abandoned the babies. Some placed unwanted babies in large earthenware pots in a public area, where strangers found them and raised them as slaves.

become citizens, but once freed, they shared the rights of the population of resident foreigners. But many slaves lived miserable lives in the mills, where they ground flour. And an estimated twenty thousand slaves labored as miners at Laureum, in southern Athens. They worked in chains day and night, lying on their backs to chisel silver ore out of the rock.

In a wealthy family, house slaves *(right)* helped do most of the household chores.

War and Feasts

Social and religious festivals played an important role in the public life of Athens. One of the city's major festivals was the Panathenaic festival held every four years in honor of the goddess Athena. People dressed up and traveled through the streets of Athens in a special procession accompanied by singers and musicians playing pipes. Athenian women wove a vast new robe for the great statue of Athena. People hung the robe over the mast of a ship, which was dragged through the city on rollers. The procession wound its way up the Panathenaic Way, the road to the Acropolis.

The festival also included footraces and chariot races. Contestants performed the dangerous feat of jumping on and off a quickly moving chariot. The Panathenaic festival concluded with the sacrifice of a cow, a sheep, or a goat. Priests left some meat for the gods. The meat was cooked and then eaten by the rest of the Athenians.

But trouble was never far away. By the 500s, the Persian Empire had engulfed much of Asia Minor (modern-day Turkey and Syria). Athens's leaders knew that the Persians would try to conquer their city. War was inevitable. In 490 B.C., the Athenian army faced a huge force of Persians at the battle of Marathon.

The Hoplite Soldiers

Athens's army was made up of its citizens. The hoplites were the infantry (foot soldiers). Most soldiers were probably prosperous farmers who could take only a few days at a time from working in their fields. Because the soldiers were unpaid, a hoplite had to be able to afford his own armor and weapons. He also had to be fit, tough, and able to carry a fifty-pound shield. The hoplites wore heavy body armor and helmets.

The hoplites fought in groups called phalanxes. Soldiers in a phalanx stood so close together that they seemed to create a wall of spears and shields. If a soldier fell, the one behind him took his place because any break would leave the entire phalanx vulnerable to the enemy.

The hoplites at the front stabbed at the enemy with their spears and swords. The soldiers at the back pushed as hard as they could, forcing the phalanx forward into the enemy army. A war was usually

The Greeks and Persians meet in bloody combat at Marathon *(left)*. A cavalryman (mounted warrior) is shown at right.

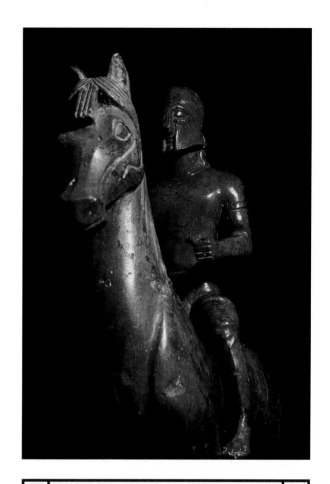

decided by a single battle in which the soldiers fought to keep control of the battleground. The army that ran away or whose force was destroyed lost.

Hoplites weren't the only soldiers. Some men served as "light-armed men"— attendants to the hoplites. They carried the hoplites' shields and baggage. As fighters, they carried a javelin of their own, along with bows and arrows. During battles, they guarded the camps from sneak attacks and helped slaughter any wounded enemy soldiers.

A citizen who could afford a horse could serve as a cavalryman in battle. Athenian horses were not very fast, so the cavalry escaped the worst of the battle.

About twenty thousand Persian forces prepared to invade Athens in 490 B.C. Athens's forces met them at Marathon, a stretch of land between mountains and sea that lay 26 miles from the city. A force of ten thousand Athenian hoplites raced across the plain toward the Persian soldiers. The hoplites killed more than six thousand Persians that day in close combat. About two hundred Athenians were killed, although thousands were wounded. Athens was then safe from invasion—for a while.

Men at Arms

Because the Greek word *hopla* means "arms," it is fitting that the hoplite soldiers were clad in armor. Their armor included a bronze helmet topped with a crest of horsehair or feathers, a bronze breastplate called a cuirass, bronze leg plates called greaves, and a large, round shield made of metal and several layers of heavy bull's hide. The hoplite carried a six-foot-long lance and a vicious, double-edged sword.

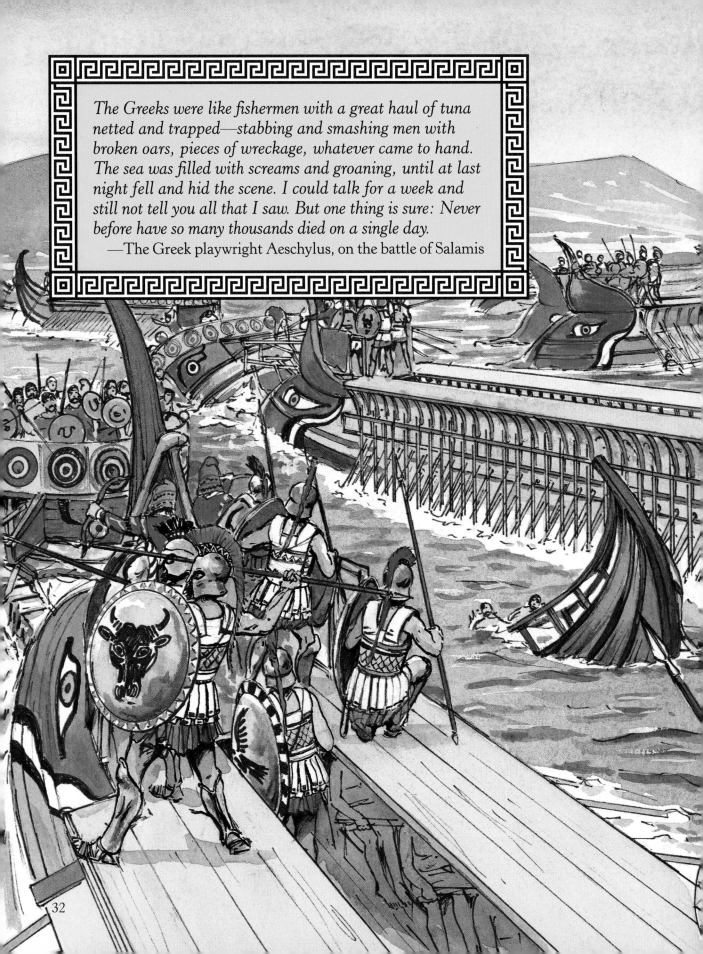

The Greeks were like fishermen with a great haul of tuna netted and trapped—stabbing and smashing men with broken oars, pieces of wreckage, whatever came to hand. The sea was filled with screams and groaning, until at last night fell and hid the scene. I could talk for a week and still not tell you all that I saw. But one thing is sure: Never before have so many thousands died on a single day.
—The Greek playwright Aeschylus, on the battle of Salamis

Masters of the Sea

lthough they had defeated the Persian army at Marathon, the Athenians knew that their enemy would try again. So they began building a huge and powerful fleet of triremes—narrow, easily maneuvered battleships with sails. Each battleship had two or three levels of oars below deck, which allowed oarsmen to row during combat. A typical warship held 170 oarsmen, 13 sailors, and a dozen soldiers and officers.

In 480 B.C., a Persian prince named Xerxes amassed a huge army and prepared to attack northern Greece. Before the battle, the Athenians consulted a religious oracle (fortune-teller) for advice on winning the war. The oracle responded, "Athens will be saved by her wooden walls." The Athenian leader Themistocles believed that this meant Athens would be saved by her wooden ships. Themistocles and the Athenian ships trapped the Persian fleet near the island of Salamis, and the Greeks easily defeated the Persians again.

But the city did not escape damage. Most Athenians had been evacuated from the city before the battle, except for a few who stayed on the Acropolis to guard the city. When the Persians surrounded the Acropolis, the Athenians rolled stones and pieces of columns down the sides of the hill. But the Persians discovered a narrow stairway leading from a cave to the hill. They burst in through the stairwell, butchered these Athenians, and set the temples on fire. A few months after the battle at Salamis, armies of the Greek city-states beat the Persians for good. Although the Persian Empire remained a world power, Athens was safe.

Athens at its Height

By the 450s, a statesman named Pericles led Athens. He was an able military leader and a politician of great influence. Pericles ordered temples, statues, and artwork to be constructed. He embellished the Agora and commissioned the Parthenon, a massive temple to Athena. The Parthenon united the Athenians in pride for their city.

From 447 to 431 B.C., Athens experienced her Golden Age. Other Greek city-states looked to Athens for leadership and protection. Athenians made important contributions to architecture, sculpture, literature, philosophy, science, and politics. The city's great navy dominated the Aegean Sea. Trade was booming.

In 431 B.C., the neighboring city-state Sparta declared war on Athens. Sparta was a society of extreme militaristic discipline, in which the people lived under harsh conditions in preparation for war. Fearing Sparta's might, Athenians crowded behind the city walls.

Two years into the war, one-third of the population of Athens died in a plague. But the war dragged on for twenty-seven long, hard years, until 404 B.C. Sparta laid siege to the city, keeping out food. Many Athenians starved to death before finally surrendering. But even though Sparta won, the long war had devastated both city-states. The Golden Age had truly ended.

In a public funeral for the dead soldiers of Athens, Pericles gave an elegant elegy: "The sacrifice which these dead have made is now being repaid to them. I speak not of that in which their poor remains are laid, but of that in which their glory survives. For the whole earth is the sepulcher [tomb] of famous men, not only are they commemorated by columns and inscriptions in their own country, but in foreign lands there dwells also an unwritten memorial of them, graven not on stone but in the hearts of men."

Athens thrived during the time of Pericles. While wars raged between Athens and its neighbors, the goddess Athena was said to watch over the city.

An Artisan's Life

Athens was home to several thousand pottery makers, painters, sculptors, stonemasons, and other artisans who strove to create beautiful works of art. Many artisans devoted their skill to building temples. The first temples were simple one-room structures, but over the centuries, constructions became more elaborate. In 431 B.C., Athenian artisans completed the Parthenon, a colossal temple dedicated to the goddess Athena. Oxcarts hauled 22,000 tons of white marble for the structure from Mount Pentelicon, 10 miles from Athens. Then the oxen dragged the stone up the steep Acropolis. The massive structure took sixteen years to complete.

The Parthenon's two architects, Ictinos and Callicrates, designed the building according to advanced mathematical proportions. The structure's lines were deliberately distorted, which produced an illusion of harmonious perfection. The complex building plan took great skill to create and execute.

A typical artisan (they were all men) rose at dawn to eat a breakfast of bread with olives, figs, or grapes. At 8 A.M., he arrived at the building site, where he might help unload large blocks of marble from the oxcarts. Then he stood on the scaffolding and, with many other workers, used strong ropes to help raise the blocks into position. Workers then secured the blocks with lead-coated strips of iron. After a lunch of bread, cheese, olives, and onions, workers continued to move stone blocks. Other craftsmen carved images for the temple's intricate friezes (carved decorative bands). At day's end, the artisan probably headed to a gymnasium for exercise and to wash himself with oil. Later, he joined his family at home for a dinner of bread, lentil soup, fruit, cheese, and wine. After the children went to bed, he would retire to the andron.

The buildings rose, matched in beauty and grace, while the workers vied with one another in the skill of their craftsmanship.
—Plutarch

School Days

During the Golden Age, education was important to Athenian society. Once girls turned seven, they were taught a little reading and writing by their mothers. They also taught girls to weave, spin, embroider, cook, and how to host dinner parties. Athenians believed that these skills would help the girls become good wives later on.

Almost all boys attended school. Boys from wealthy families had private tutors (from whom their sisters might also learn). Other boys went to school at a teacher's home. Education wasn't mandatory in Athens, but people viewed a father who didn't send his son to school with a great deal of contempt.

In most schoolrooms, students sat on low, wooden benches. They wrote on wax

Scenes from an ancient Greek school day. Teachers in yellow and students in red are captured on pottery *(right)*.

tablets with the blunt end of a stylus, a penlike stick that scored the wax. To erase the tablet, a writer would warm it over a fire. A teacher sat on a high chair at the front of the room. If a student misbehaved, he could expect the teacher to flog him with a rod or a lash.

The Athenian system of education developed the student's entire character. Instructors taught fairness and politeness in addition to reading, writing, athletics, and music. Boys learned some simple arithmetic, but only students studying to be bankers learned more complicated math. Most grown men used their fingers or small pebbles to add and subtract. Students also memorized long passages of the *Iliad* and the *Odyssey.* They stood by their chairs and repeated after the teacher as he read lines from Homer's epics.

> *The direction in which education starts a man will determine his future life.*
> —Plato

Athens's Great Minds

The Greeks are credited with inventing philosophy, a word that translates to "a love of wisdom." Athenian men spent hours in the Agora discussing the mysteries of life and the world around them. Some Athenians made a career out of the pursuit of wisdom. Traveling teachers, called "sophists," used clever reasoning to make people think in new ways.

Socrates was one of Athens's greatest thinkers and teachers. He taught by relentlessly questioning his students, forcing them to think of answers for themselves. Socrates lived a simple life and refused payment for his teaching. But powerful Athenians felt his teachings challenged their authority. In 399 B.C., Socrates was condemned to death and forced to drink a cup of hemlock (poison).

One of Socrates' students, Plato, was another great Athenian philosopher. Plato wrote down much of Socrates' teachings and called his teacher "the wisest and most just and best man" who ever lived. Aristotle traveled from his home of Macedonia (in northern Greece) to study at Plato's school, the Academy. Aristotle became a gifted scientist and scholar who tutored a Macedonian prince named Alexander.

> *Athenians, I am not going to argue for my own sake...but for yours, that you may not sin against the God by condemning me, who am his gift to you. For if you kill me you will not easily find a successor to me....*
> —Socrates, speaking to the judges who sentenced him to death for his teachings

His many accomplishments did not protect Socrates from being ordered to drink poison *(left)*. But he left behind a legacy picked up by his students, shown in this Roman mosaic *(right)*.

*Observe, Athenians, the height to which
the fellow's insolence has soared: he leaves
you no choice of action or inaction;...he
cannot rest content with what he has
conquered; he is always taking in more,
everywhere casting his net round us, while
we sit idle and do nothing. When, Athenians,
will you take the necessary action?*
—Demosthenes' speech against King Philip

Athens Falls to the Macedonians

North of Athens lay the kingdom of Macedonia, inhabited by people of Greek descent whom the Athenians regarded as barbarians. By 352 B.C., it was clear that the Macedonian leader, King Philip II, wanted to annex the Greek city-states into his own kingdom.

This was a tense time for Athens. Some citizens wanted to voluntarily join Macedonia, but others wanted to fight Philip. Athenian orators (expert speech makers who worked to persuade the Assembly) played a role in figuring out what Athenians should do. The Athenian orator Isocrates appealed to the citizens to join the Macedonian monarch. Demosthenes, another speaker, convinced the Assembly to fight Macedonia. Demosthenes is remembered as Athens's greatest orator.

In 338 B.C., Philip's forces defeated the Athenian army. After this victory, Philip formed the League of Corinth, encompassing the Greek city-states and Macedonia. Philip was generous and lenient to Athens, and the city continued to thrive. When Philip was murdered in 336 B.C., his son Alexander III (the Great) succeeded him. Alexander, who had been tutored by Aristotle, was a gifted leader and scholar. Alexander led his armies in a war that—again—defeated the massive Persian Empire. He conquered Asia Minor, Syria, Egypt, Mesopotamia, Babylon, Assyria, Turkistan, Afghanistan, and northwestern India. He created an empire that spread Athenian art, philosophy, literature, and political ideas to its far reaches.

In this sixteenth-century tapestry *(opposite)*, Alexander rallies his troops. A bust *(above)* captures the confidence of the young king.

Athens under Roman Rule

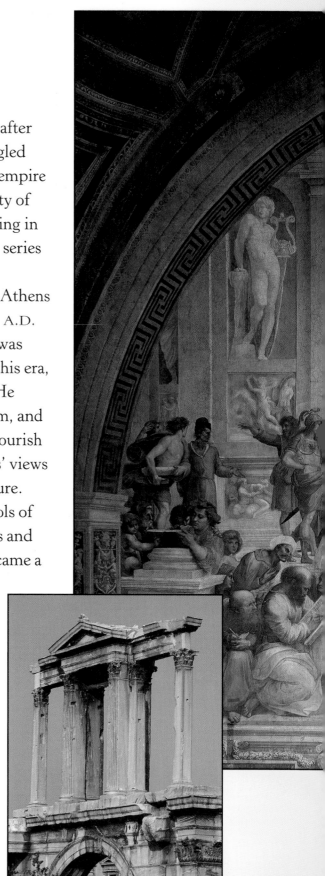

Alexander the Great died in 323 B.C. after a short illness. His successors struggled for power for twenty years, and his empire crumbled. In the meantime, the central Italian city of Rome was building an empire of its own. Beginning in 280 B.C., Rome battled the Greek city-states in a series of conflicts called the Punic Wars.

In 148 B.C., Rome annexed Greece, including Athens and Macedonia. The period between 31 B.C. and A.D. 180, known as the Pax Romana (Roman Peace), was peaceful and prosperous for Athens. For part of this era, the Roman emperor Hadrian settled in Athens. He endowed the city with a new library, a gymnasium, and a triumphal arch. Athens's culture managed to flourish and influence its conqueror, and the two cultures' views of the world blended to form Greco-Roman culture. Romans flocked to be educated in the great schools of Athens. Theater flourished, attracting Athenians and Romans alike. The port at Piraeus once again became a bustling center of trade.

Athens's population of artisans increased as people in Rome imported Athenian sculpture, marble columns, terra-cotta vases, and bronze and silver bowls and cups. Athenians expanded existing buildings and constructed new ones.

In *School of Athens*, a famous Italian Renaissance painting, Italian genius Leonardo da Vinci *(center, orange cloak)* exchanges ideas with his ancient Greek counterpart, Aristotle *(on da Vinci's right)*. Roman emperors left their mark on Athens, such as this arched gate *(left)*, commissioned by the emperor Hadrian.

A Day at the Theater

Theater was a central part of Athenian social life, and it soon became popular with Roman visitors to Athens. The concept of theater grew out of the Athenian religious festival of Dionysus, the god of wine. Theatrical performances took place on a bare hillside until artisans built a large stone arena, called an amphitheater, into the hillside near the Acropolis in A.D. 340.

Many Greek plays featured three actors and a chorus of singers and dancers, who offered commentary and narrated offstage events. The actors wore elaborate masks and high shoes to make them more visible to distant audience members. Because women weren't permitted to perform, the masks made it easier for men to act female roles.

Audience members brought baskets of food. Many came with pillows to cushion the stone seats. If the audience enjoyed the show, they shouted, *"Authis! Authis!"* which means "Again! Again!" They hooted and threw date pits and small pebbles at bad actors.

Masks depicting raw emotions *(inset)* were worn by classical Greek actors, who performed on magnificent outdoor stages in Athens *(right)*.

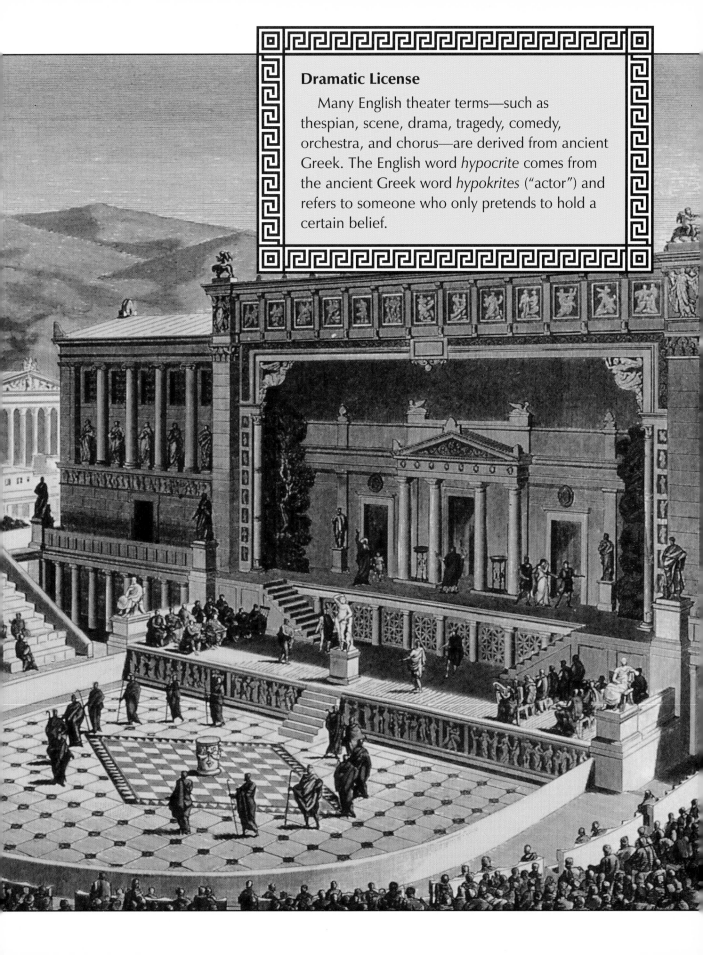

Dramatic License

Many English theater terms—such as thespian, scene, drama, tragedy, comedy, orchestra, and chorus—are derived from ancient Greek. The English word *hypocrite* comes from the ancient Greek word *hypokrites* ("actor") and refers to someone who only pretends to hold a certain belief.

Athens Becomes Christian

In A.D. 49, the Christian apostle Paul brought Christianity to Athens. In 313 the Roman emperor Constantine the Great officially Christianized the Roman Empire with the Edict of Milan. In 330 Constantine moved his empire's capital from Rome to Byzantium, a former Greek colony on the horn of Asia Minor. The city became known as Constantinople in the emperor's honor, and the empire was called the Byzantine Empire.

Greek culture played a major role in the rise of Christianity. The Bible's New Testament was written in Greek, early church services were conducted in Greek, and many of the early church fathers were Greek. Athenian farmers raised animals and crops that fed the Byzantine Empire. They paid taxes to the emperor to support his extravagant court and helped support his army. The taxes also supported the church clergy.

Christianity transformed Athens. In 394 Emperor Theodosius I closed some of

the city's schools and temples because they weren't Christian. He allowed some temples to remain open. He also stopped the Olympic Games. But Athens remained the cultural capital of the Greek world until 529. In that year, the emperor Justinian I closed down the Academy (established by Plato), and outlawed the teaching of philosophy. Wealthy Romans no longer sent their youngsters to be educated in Greece.

The great Parthenon had been converted from a temple to the goddess Athena into a Christian church. All across Athens, workers erected Byzantine churches in a style that blended Middle Eastern and Roman architecture. The structures featured domes, mosaics, carvings, and columns.

The Christian churches in Rome and Constantinople (the eastern capital of the empire) split in 1054. Athens's Orthodox Church, founded in the 400s, became even more central to Greek society and culture.

A Byzantine Christian church *(left)* stands on the site of the ancient Agora. Icons, such as this one of Saint Michael the Archangel *(inset)*, often lined the walls of such churches.

Village Life

The Middle Ages were a difficult time for Athenians. Possession of the city passed from the Byzantine Empire to a series of invaders. From 1205 to 1311, Franks controlled Athens. Between 1311 and 1402, the city was ruled by the Catalans, the Florentines, and the Venetians.

Through the Middle Ages, the city became less important and shrank in population. Most Athenians lived quiet, simple lives. Women helped their husbands tend fields, where they grew traditional crops, such as vegetables, olives, and grapes. They used handheld tools like hoes, sickles, and scythes. The men of the household fished using homemade nets and fish traps. Before heading out in their boats, they offered up prayers to a local Christian saint charged with protecting fishermen. Women cooked for their families and baked bread in large outdoor ovens, which served several families. They spun and wove wool to make their families' clothes.

Most Athenians adopted the clothing styles of the Byzantine Empire. Men wore long, loose-fitting coats. Women wound scarves around their heads, letting the scarf ends fall over their shoulders, and they chose simple tunics covered by loose, hooded cloaks. Villagers lived in whitewashed, one-room homes made of sun-dried bricks and held together by wooden beams covered with straw, dirt, and grass. Each house had a courtyard and a barn outside.

Athenians adopted the Byzantine practice of sitting at tables in chairs. They worshiped in local Christian churches.

51

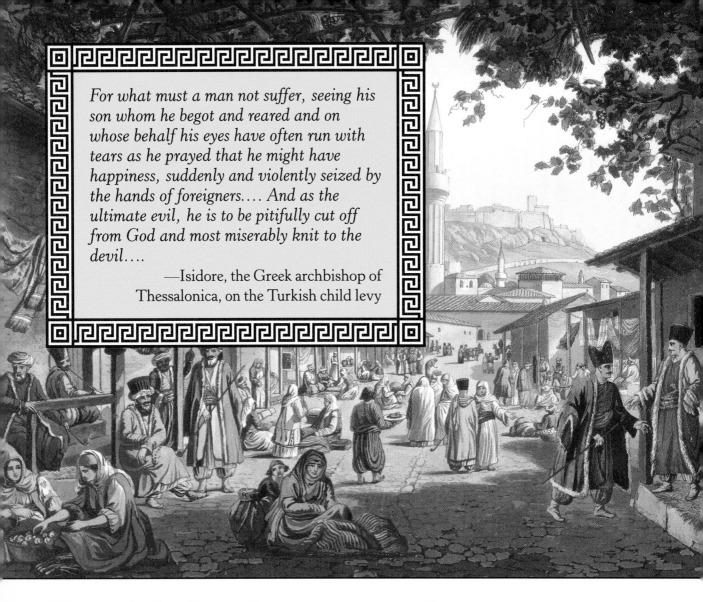

For what must a man not suffer, seeing his son whom he begot and reared and on whose behalf his eyes have often run with tears as he prayed that he might have happiness, suddenly and violently seized by the hands of foreigners.... And as the ultimate evil, he is to be pitifully cut off from God and most miserably knit to the devil....

—Isidore, the Greek archbishop of Thessalonica, on the Turkish child levy

Turkish Occupation

In 1453 the Turkish Ottoman Empire conquered the Byzantine Empire and captured Constantinople. The Turks were Muslim nomadic people. They had moved westward from central Asia into eastern Europe over hundreds of years.

After a two-year-long siege, Athens fell to the Ottoman forces in 1456. The conquerors converted the Parthenon into a mosque (Islamic house of worship) around 1466. Many Athenians converted to Islam. The poor converted in hopes of improving their economic situation. The wealthy converted in hopes of keeping their power and their land.

Many Athenians converted to avoid the child levy. Every four or five years, the

When the Ottoman Empire took over Athens, minarets (mosque towers) rose above the skyline, as seen in this nineteenth-century painting *(left)*. Athenians who converted to Islam worshiped in mosques with Turkish Muslims *(above)*.

Turkish government took the brightest and healthiest Athenian boys.

The boys were raised as Muslim Turks and were trained to serve the sultan (king) in his imperial palace or as soldiers in the fierce Ottoman army. Many boys benefited from a good education and a comfortable existence. But few families saw their abducted sons again, so parents resisted the practice. Some even bought boys from needy Turkish neighbors who wanted their sons to have good lives as Ottoman soldiers.

The Ottoman Empire allowed Athenians to continue practicing Christianity if they paid a special tax. Some sultans forbade Christians to build churches, to carry arms, or to dress like Muslims. Many Christian men left Athens to become monks in mountain communities. There they studied and copied ancient religious manuscripts.

Fight for Freedom

Under Ottoman rule, Athens had degenerated into a crowded, insignificant town. By the 1500s, African pirates working for the Ottoman sultan had captured thousands of Greeks to work in Constantinople or to be sold into the international slave trade. In 1688 so many Athenians fled to the nearby island of Salamis that the city was deserted for nearly three years. By the 1700s, the huge Ottoman Empire had begun to crumble. The sultans were unable to control their vast territory. As the empire fell, Athens's intellectual life began to reawaken. Greek merchants once again came to dominate trade in the Mediterranean. Athenians grew more and more restless under Turkish occupation.

A spirit of independence was in the air, and Greek rebels began to seek freedom from the Ottoman Empire. Many were inspired by the American Revolution and the French Revolution, which began in

The sea brings the pirate galleys of the barbarians who in their turn bring with them fearful captivity and fresh cause for lamentation…. Families scattered to the far extremes of foreign soil, the dearest possession of our nation became the spoils of barbarian violence and the wealth, which Athens once won by the spear, loaded to the waterline the ships of the infidels.
—Athenian spokesman Argyrus Bernades, 1659–1720

1789. In 1821 influential Greek church officers, led by Archbishop Germanos, initiated a rebellion of Greek peasants. Athenians and other Greeks fought with scythes, clubs, and slings. Many on both sides died. Seagoing Greek merchants turned their ships against the Turks. Greek sailors drafted into the Ottoman navy deserted to join the rebellion. The Greek War of Independence had begun.

On land, Egypt fortified the Turks with ten thousand troops. By 1827 it was clear that the Greeks were losing. Russia, Britain, and France offered Greece their aid. On October 20, 1827, the Turks and Egyptians were defeated at the Bay of Navarino. In 1832 the British, French, and Russians guaranteed independence to a new Greek state. The Bavarian prince Otto, son of King Louis I of Bavaria, took the throne to become King Otto I.

In 1834 Athens became the capital of Greece in honor of the city's historic greatness. At that time, the worn-out, devastated city of Athens had only eight thousand residents. Few buildings had survived the war, but the stage was set for a renaissance.

After Independence

Between 1834, when Athens became the capital of
Greece, and 1947, the nation doubled its territory.
Greece was involved in both world wars. Italians and
Germans captured Greece, and Athenians suffered under Nazi
occupation from 1941 to 1944. After World War II, Greece
endured a civil war from 1946 to 1949. As the capital, Athens fell
into political and economic shambles. In 1967 a military coup led
to a reign of terror by brutal secret police. Democracy was restored
in 1974, and the monarchy was officially dissolved.

Modern-day Greece is a parliamentary republic. A president
serves as head of state and a prime minister heads the government.
Athens is a busy metropolis of more than three million inhabitants
and is an important European capital.

Low houses with balconies line twisting streets. Ancient olive
trees stand in courtyards, and grapevines twist around doorways.
Farmers continue to grow olives and grapes as well as tobacco, figs,
barley, wheat, and rice. Many Athenians are great fishers and
sailors. Their diet is similar to that of ancient times, centering on
grapes, olives, eggplant, fish, cheese, stuffed grape leaves, pastry,
and wine. Athenians enjoy strong coffee, which became
an important feature of Greek meals in Ottoman times.

In open-air markets, vendors sell everything from fruit,
vegetables, fresh eggs, and doughnut-shaped bread (called
koulouria) to soap, T-shirts, shoes, sea sponges, jewelry, and tools.
Shoppers can even find spare car parts.

Athenians value hard work but also like eating out, spending
time with friends, and going to the theater. People often arrive late
to social engagements. Instead of listing starting times of movies,
theaters post a synopsis so that latecomers can catch up with a
film's plot. Athenians rest every afternoon, when many businesses
and public buildings close for a few hours.

Outdoor cafés in Athens *(above)* line the twisting streets in commercial areas.

Modern Athens

Ancient and modern lie side-by-side in Athens. Plays in the amphitheater draw crowds. Cars scoot through ancient triumphal arches. Orthodoxy is the official Greek religion, and the Greek Orthodox Church is an important part of life in Athens. Most Athenian babies are baptized, and the church is host to most weddings and funerals. People stop into church before work to light a candle and to say a prayer. At lunchtime Orthodox priests may shop for food or meet with friends. In their black robes, cylindrical hats, and long beards, the priests remind passersby of their rich cultural past. These days Athens draws millions of visitors familiar with Greek literature, art,

Tourists crowd the Parthenon *(left)*. A Greek Orthodox priest leaves an ancient chapel sheltered by a modern skyscraper *(above)*.

philosophy, and architecture. Athens's economy relies on the tourist industry, but the heavy influx of visitors is taking its toll. The foundations of ancient monuments such as the Parthenon slowly deteriorate from the vibrations of so many visitors' feet. Pollution and smog are destructive, too. During the twentieth century, the city's buildings eroded more than in the previous twenty-four centuries. Sulphur dioxide from industry and car exhaust combine with moisture in the air to create acid that eats at buildings' marble surfaces.

During Athens's Golden Age, Pericles remarked: "What I desire is that you fix your eyes every day on the greatness of Athens and fall in love with her.... Mighty indeed are the marks and monuments of our empire which we have left. Future ages will wonder at us, as the present age wonders at us now." His words have more than proven true.

Athens Timeline

Second Millennium B.C.	First Millennium B.C.

1900 B.C. to 800 B.C.
Early History

1900 B.C.	Mycenaeans first occupy Attica
1600–1450 B.C.	Mycenaeans dominate and intermarry with Minoans of Crete
1250 B.C.	Mycenaeans found Athens atop Acropolis
1200 B.C.	The Greek Dark Ages begin
ca.1100 B.C.	Dorians invade Greece and refugees flood Athens

800 B.C. to 500 B.C.
The Rise of Athens

800 B.C.	Athens emerges from the Dark Ages
776 B.C.	First Olympic Games held
CA. 700 B.C.	Homeric epics recorded; Athens begins colonization beyond Greek peninsula
682 B.C.	Monarchy is replaced by rule of archons
621 B.C.	Draco elected archon
594 B.C.	Solon elected archon
560 B.C.	Pesistratus rules as tyrant
507 B.C.	Cleisthenes introduces democracy

500 B.C. to 323 B.C.
Classical Times

490 B.C.	Greeks defeat Persians at the battle of Marathon
480–479 B.C.	Greeks defeat Persians at the battle of Salamis
470 B.C.	Socrates is born
462 B.C.	Statesman Ephialtes' reforms strip aristocratic power
447 B.C.	Athens's Golden Age
443 B.C.	Pericles elected leader of Athens
432 B.C.	The Parthenon is completed
431 B.C.	Peloponnesian War between Athens and Sparta begins
429 B.C.	Pericles dies of plague
404 B.C.	Athens surrenders to Sparta
399 B.C.	Socrates condemned to death
387 B.C.	Plato founds the Academy
342 B.C.	Aristotle begins tutoring Alexander the Great
340 B.C.	Amphitheater built in Athens
338 B.C.	King Philip II of Macedonia defeats Athens
336 B.C.	King Philip dies and Alexander the Great succeeds him

323 B.C. to A.D. 1453	**323 B.C.**	Alexander the Great dies
Hellenism Conquers	**280 B.C.**	Roman-Greek Punic Wars begin
the World	**148 B.C.**	Rome annexes Greece
	82-79 B.C.	Roman Emperor Sulla storms Athens
	31 B.C.–A.D. 180	The Pax Romana

A.D. 49	Apostle Paul preaches to Athenians
A.D. 120–128	Emperor Hadrian lives in Athens
A.D. 313	Constantine Christianizes the Roman Empire
A.D. 324	Emperor Theodosius closes schools and temples
A.D. 364	The Roman Empire is split into east and west
A.D. 400	The rise of Greek Orthodox Church
A.D. 429	The Parthenon converted to a church
A.D. 529	Emperor Justinian closes Plato's Academy
A.D. 1054	The Roman and Byzantine churches split
A.D. 1204–1225	Franks capture Constantinople and divide Greece into feudal principalities
A.D. 1311–1402	Control of Athens passes to Catalans, Florentines, and Venetians

A.D. 1453–	**A.D. 1453**	Ottoman Turks capture Constantinople, ending Byzantine Empire
The Later Years	**A.D. 1456**	Ottoman Turks conquer Athens
	A.D. 1466	The Parthenon becomes a mosque
	A.D. 1821	Greek War of Independence begins
	A.D. 1827	War ends
	A.D. 1830	Greece becomes independent nation
	A.D. 1843	Athens established as capital of Greece
	A.D. 1967	Military junta takes power
	A.D. 1974	Monarchy abolished and democracy restored
	A.D. 1991	Metropolitan Athens's population reaches 3.5 million

Books about Greece and Athens

Bowra, C. M. *Classical Greece*. New York: Time Incorporated, 1965.

Burrell, Roy. *The Greeks*. New York: Oxford University Press, 1990.

Day, Nancy. *Your Travel Guide to Ancient Greece*. Minneapolis: Runestone Press, 2001.

Dazzling! Jewelry of the Ancient World. Minneapolis: Runestone Press, 1994.

Greece in Pictures. Minneapolis: Lerner Publications Company, 1996.

Horton, Casey. *Ancient Greeks*. New York: Gloucester Press, 1984.

Ling, Roger. *The Greek World*. New York: Peter Bedrick Books, 1988.

Loverance and Wood. *Ancient Greece*. New York: The Penguin Group, 1992.

Macdonald, Fiona. *A Greek Temple*. New York: Peter Bedrick Books, 1992.

Nardo, Don. *Life in Ancient Greece*. San Diego: Lucent Books, 1996.

Nicholson, Robert. *Ancient Greece*. New York: Chelsea House Publishers, 1994.

Pearson, Anne. *Ancient Greece*. New York: Alfred A. Knopf, 1992.

Piece by Piece! Mosaics of the Ancient World. Minneapolis: Runestone Press, 1993.

Powell, Anton. *Ancient Greece*. New York: Facts on File, Inc., 1989.

Robinson, Charles Alexander Jr. *Ancient Greece*. New York: Franklin Watts, 1984.

Stewart, Philippa. *Growing Up in Ancient Greece*. London: B.T. Batsford, Ltd., 1980.

Woods, Michael, and Mary B. Woods. *Ancient Machines*. Minneapolis: Runestone Press, 2000.

Index

Academy, the, 40–41

Acropolis, 6, 7, 8, 12, 33

Alexander the Great, 5, 40, 42–43, 44

Aphrodite, 13

Apollo, 13

archons, 18–19

Areopagus, 18–19

Ares, 13

Aristotle, 10, 40–41

Artemis, 13

artisans, 36–37, 44–45

Assembly, the, 2

Athena, 12, 13, 28
    statue of, 12

athletics, 16, 28–29

boule, the, 21

Byzantine Empire, 49, 51

cavalry, 30–31

child levy system, 52

children, 26–27, 38–39

chitons, 22–23

Christianity, 48–49, 51, 52–53

Circe, 15

citizenship, 21

clothing, 22–23

Constantine the Great, 49

construction, 36–37

cooking, 26–27

cosmetics, 22

Crete, 6

Cyclops, 15

Dark Ages, 7

Demeter, 13

democracy, 5, 18, 21

Demosthenes, 42–43

diet, 10, 36

Dionysus, 13, 46–47

Dorians, 7

Draco, 18

Edict of Milan, 49

education, 24, 38–39, 49

farming, 10, 18, 50–51, 56

festivals, 28–29

games, 16–17

Germanos, Archbishop, 55

gods, 12

Golden Age, 34

government, 5, 18–19, 21

Greek Orthodox Church, 58

Greek War of Independence, 55

Hadrian, 44

Helen of Troy, 15

Hephaestus, 13

Hera, 13

Heraia, the, 16

Hermes, 13

Hill of Ares, 18

himations, 22–23

Homer, 15

hoplites, 30–31

housing, 8, 24–25

Iliad, the, 15, 39

Islam, 52–53

Isocrates, 43

janissaries, 53

Justinian, 49

League of Corinth, 43

Louis I, King, 55

Macedonia, 43

Marathon, 31, 33

Marathon, Battle of, 29

marketplaces, 8, 26–27, 56

Middle Ages, 51

mining, 26

Mount Olympus, 12

music, 14

Mycenaeans, 6, 15

mythology, 12

Odyssey, the, 15, 39

Olympic Games, 16, 49

orphans, 26

Ottoman Empire, 52–53, 54–55

Parthenon, 12, 34–35, 49, 52, 58–59

Pax Romana, the, 44

Pericles, 34–35

Persian Empire, 29, 33

phalanxes, 30

Philip II, King, 5, 42–43

philosophy, 40–41

Piraeus, 10, 44

Plato, 49

Pnyx, 21

pollution, 59

Poseidon, 13

religion, 6, 12–13, 28–29, 32–33

Rome, 44

sailing, 10, 32–33, 54–55, 56

Salamis, Battle of, 33

School of Athens, 45

sirens, 15

slaves, 26–27, 55

Socrates, 40

soldiers, 30–31, 52–53

Solon, 18–19

Sparta, 35

Stone Age, 6

storytelling, 12, 14–15

theater, 44, 46–47

trade, 10

Trojan War, 15

weapons, 30–31

weaving, 22, 51

weddings, 24–25

World War II, 56

Xerxes, 33

Zeus, 13

About the Author and Illustrator

Dawn Kotapish is a writer and editor living in Oak Park, Illinois. She has traveled widely throughout the Mediterranean and the Middle East and lived for a number of years in Saudi Arabia. She has worked as an English teacher in Chicago, in West Africa, and in Nepal. She also is the author of *Daily Life in Ancient and Modern Baghdad,* another title in the *Cities through Time* series.

Bob Moulder of Derby, England, studied art in Belfast, Northern Ireland. He is a specialist in historical artwork and comic strips. He is an accomplished author of history books, and his artwork has appeared in leading publications in the United Kingdom.

Acknowledgments

For quoted material: pp. 10, 24 Nardo, Don. *Life in Ancient Greece.*(San Diego: Lucent Books, 1996); p. 19 *The World of Athens.* (Joint Association of Classical Teacher's Greek Course Background Book. Cambridge: Cambridge University Press, 1984); p. 20 Ling, Roger. *The Making of the Past: The Greek World.* (New York: Peter Bedrick Books, 1988); p. 32 Loverance and Wood. *Ancient Greece.* (New York: The Penguin Group, 1992); pp. 35, 45 Crow, John A. *Greece: The Magic Spring.* (New York: Harper and Row Publishers, 1970); p. 37 MacDonald, Fiona. *A Greek Temple.* (New York: Peter Bedrick Books, 1992); p. 39 Bartlett, John. *Familiar Quotations, 14th edition.* (Little, Brown, and Co., Boston, 1968); pp. 40, 42 Bowra, C. M. *Classical Greece.* (New York: Time Incorporated, 1965); pp. 52 , 54 Zakythinos, D. A.*The Making of Modern Greece: From Byzantium to Independence.* (Totowa, NJ: Rowman and Littlefield, 1976); p. 59 Davenport, William Wyatt. *Athens. (*Amsterdam: Time-Life Books, 1978).

For photographs and art reproductions: The Stock Market, p. 4; North Wind Picture Archives, pp. 10–11,18-19, 27, 30, 38-39, 46-47; National Archaeological Museum, Athens/Bridgeman Art Library, London/New York, p. 12; Nimatallah/Art Resource, New York, p. 13; AKG Photo, London/Wener Forman Archive, British Museum, London, pp. 16–17; Art Resource, New York, pp. 17, 41; Galleria Ufizzi, Florence/Art Resource, New York, p. 18; Louvre, Paris/Art Resource, New York, pp. 22–23; The Granger Collection, New York, pp. 31, 34–35; Alinari/Art Resource, New York, p. 40; Avignon, France/Silvio Fiore/SuperStock, p. 42; Staatliche Glypothek, Munich, Germany/ET Archive, London/SuperStock, p. 43; Gian Berto Vanni, Athens/Art Resource, New York, p. 44; Erich Lessing/Art Resource, New York, pp. 44–45; Mary Evans Picture Library, London, pp. 46, 54-55; Dave Toht, Greenleaf Publishing, Inc., pp. 48, 58-59 (both); Corbis Images, Bellvue, p. 49; Bridgeman Art Library, London/New York, pp. 52–53; Corbis Images, Bellvue, pp. 56–57; Cover: The Granger Collection, New York